Contrast

THE DESIGN CONCEPT SERIES

Contrast

Jack Selleck

Art Teacher, Emerson Junior High School
Los Angeles, California

DAVIS PUBLICATIONS, INC.
Worcester, Massachusetts U.S.A.

To my daughter, Lisa, a sensitive and good person

Spatial Construction, acrylic on linen. Artist, Rinaldo Paluzzi. Silvan Simone Gallery, Los Angeles. Bold, angled dark and light forms contrast with each other and with the circular shape.

Copyright 1975
Davis Publications, Inc.
Worcester, Massachusetts U.S.A.

Printed in the United States of America
Library of Congress Catalog Card Number: 75-21110
ISBN 0-87192-074-3

Printing: Davis Press, Inc.
Binding: A. Horowitz & Son
Type: Optima Medium
Graphic Design: Penny Darras, Thumbnail Associates

Consulting Editors: Gerald F. Brommer, George F. Horn, Sarita R. Rainey

10   9   8   7   6   5   4   3   2

Contents

Introduction

PERSONALITY, EMOTION, CREATIVITY

Our lives are filled with emotional and visual contrasts—the joy we may see and feel at a wedding of friends, or the sadness we sense when a pet is ill or helpless.

We see contrasts in nature—dramatic stripes of a zebra, the bright features of a male bird. We see contrasts in our cities and towns—old houses being torn down and new buildings going up.

After eating a hamburger, we might have a dish of ice cream, not necessarily because we're still hungry, but partly because of the pleasurable contrast of the taste.

Sometimes our mood and the situation can determine whether we're exhilarated and happy being part of a large crowd or frustrated and anxious to get away and have some peaceful moments to gather our thoughts.

Many other contrasts affect our lives and help shape our personalities. Contrasts are endless in number and difficult to measure as to their degree of influence on us.

All of us need variety and contrasts in the things we see and do. Artists, film-makers, musicians, authors and dancers use contrasts in their work to add variety, change the pace, or develop or emphasize a mood.

Artists may be directly influenced by contrasts, whether subtle like the different greens seen in a forest, or more dramatic like the light and shadow patterns of early morning. Even more profound contrasts can be found in the happy or tragic events of our lives.

The work of some artists may be abstract or non-objective and still be influenced (perhaps subconsciously) by contrasts that exist in the real world.

The force, and even anger, of a powerful brush stroke may be the extension of one painter's concern for his fellow man, or his interest may be chiefly in the brush stroke itself as the paint contrasts with another color or the white canvas.

Awareness of these subtle to dramatic contrasts adds to our understanding of life, ourselves and each other as we communicate with our words, gestures and creative efforts. Hopefully, this book will be a step towards furthering this awareness.

Students "ham it up" for the camera. On the opposite
page, a solitary, lonely youth is seen in a painting where
the artist has used many contrasts to emphasize the
mood.

Desolation: Boy in Empty Room, Walter Stuempfig. Oil
on canvas, 30'' by 25''. Los Angeles County Museum of
Art, Estate of Clifton Webb.

Debbie's Room. Most of us have favorite objects that we've gathered—to bring back fond memories, to look at or touch, or to have handy when we need to use them.

Some artists use these kinds of objects and perhaps add their own drawing, painting and imaginative combinations to produce assemblages or constructions. This one is by Gordon Wagner. Note the three-dimensional trains with puffs of "cotton smoke." The lower train is a painting. Photography by Jim Goss.

Some artists deal with emotional themes in their work. Others use techniques that in themselves show great emotion.

Slashing and smeared brush strokes help emphasize this college student's painting of an angry person.

George Grosz, an artist concerned with the plight of his fellow-man, contrasted varied line thicknesses, broken and flowing lines and brushed-in ink areas to add vitality and a sense of urgency to this drawing. Note the gestures and expressions of the figures.

Even in this "abstracted" detail of the man's coat we can see active and strong contrasts.

Street Scene 1931/32, George Grosz. Black ink and white brush drawing, 18½" x 23¼". Los Angeles County Museum of Art, Mr. and Mrs. William Preston Harrison Collection.

12

Contrast: Natural and Man-Made

Natural and man-made objects can be seen in interesting combinations around us—in dramatic, subtle, and even humorous contrasts.

The designers of this house used man-made cement blocks contrasted with natural rock, wood, shrubs and trees. Too much contrast can be visually confusing, whether in a house or a work of art.

An old house near the beach has lost the battle against wind, dampness, sun and progress.

An excellent example of natural and man-made partnership can be seen in the Anasazi Indian dwellings in Arizona's Canyon de Chelly. The natural rock formations provided protection from intruders and the weather.

David Smith's geometric and abstract sculpture contrasts dramatically with the natural, large pine trees in the background.

The geometric design on the wall of this building needed to be "softened," so as not to appear too massive and sterile. The natural plants will do the job as they develop and grow.

The natural, free-forming cobweb provides a delicate contrast to the vertical and horizontal latticework.

There is an almost humorous aspect to the contrast between man's telephone pole and nature's tree in this photo. Both seem to be trying to outdo each other as wires and branches reach out.

Sometimes a necessary utilitarian object like this fire hydrant can be made less of an eyesore if surrounded by some greenery. Interesting contrast exists between the heavy, strong, stationary metal hydrant and the delicate flowers and growing plants.

A newly planted tree looks wistfully lost against the massive concrete freeway structure. Landscaping along these freeways is necessary to keep our cities from becoming "concrete monsters."

The roof structure of an open patio combines with a natural plant. Trees reflecting in the window also add a harmonious touch.

Stick-Up 1972, Chuck Arnoldi. Los Angeles County Museum of Art. A design made of tree branches and enamel, 81″ x 81″.

A wagon wheel of wood and metal, made by man, rests against nature's tree.

Nature provided the flowers and sunlight, and man the glass vase and window in this simple but beautiful arrangement.

Contrast in Materials

Man puts together different materials to make many things—things to use every day, things for fun and leisure and works of art to see and enjoy. They may be as simple as a chair or as complicated as a modern building.

Metal, wood, paint, bricks and trees are combined for strength and visual enticement at this amusement park.

Textured fabric contrasts with smooth, thin but sturdy metal. Notice the interesting shapes within the basic design. Permission to photograph by Knoll International, Los Angeles.

The bench (above right) incorporates figures into the structure. Decorated areas contrast with plain areas. Permission to photograph by Silvan Simone Gallery, Los Angeles. Artist, Altina Carey.

3-DIMENSIONAL ART WORK

The General. An empty plastic bottle was used for the head, a piece of felt for the hat and a broken desk seat for the body. Eyes from a magazine, medals of paint refills and bottle caps add detail.

Inside a cardboard box, a somber figure surveys the aftermath of a fire. Paint, paper, sticks, cellophane and wire were combined in a dramatic way.

Pen caps, collage and the artist's own drawing and painting were combined in this simple but strong design.

All projects on these two pages are by Emerson Junior High students.

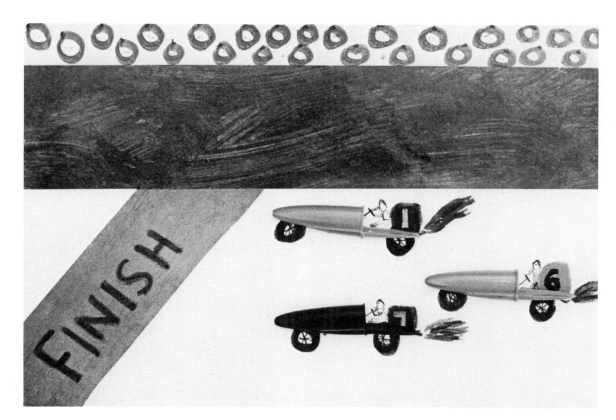

This chair, with a cellophane and rattan back, seems almost capable of "flying off" with the small balsa figure.

Broken records, tin, leatherette, a sprayer and other
odds and ends were incorporated in this motorcycle
assemblage mounted on wood.

Both projects by Emerson Junior High Students.

Construction for Noble Ladies 1919, Kurt Schwitters, German, 1887-1948. Mixed Media Assemblage, wood, metal, paint, 33" x 40½". Los Angeles County Museum of Art, Museum Purchase Fund. The angled wood and circular shapes contrast to give a sense of movement. The different textures add visual interest as well.

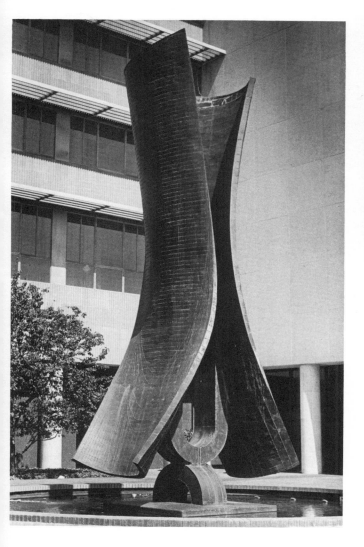

Sweet William 1962, John Chamberlain. Metal, welded. and painted sculpture, 46" width x 69" height x 62" length. Los Angeles County Museum of Art. Gift of Mr. and Mrs. Abe Adler in memory of Mrs. Esther Steif Rosen through the Contemporary Art Council. Crushed, bent and twisted metal stands like a powerful force, thrusting and balancing and maintaining a sense of strength and dignity.

Many firms and companies are calling on artists to make large, impressive works of art: murals, sculptures and fountains. The use and contrast of materials is often exciting to view. Our eye may "slide" over glass, "bounce off" light and dark areas or dwell on a highly textured detail of wood, stone or metal.

29

Contrast in the Mind

Suspended Book (Crackers) 1970, Edward Ruscha. Gunpowder and pastel on paper, drawing, 29″ x 11½″. Los Angeles County Museum of Art, Gift of Contemporary Art Council.

Though some type of contrast exists in most scenes or artworks, there is often a stronger contrast that exists more in the mind. In the picture above, a single object is contrasted against a larger, empty area, but the crucial contrast is the floating book and its shadow—our mind compares this to the way we normally see a book.

Many contrasts exist in this wall painting—color, shapes, dark and light. But it is the strange image of buildings going into space, seemingly through other buildings, that plays on the mind.

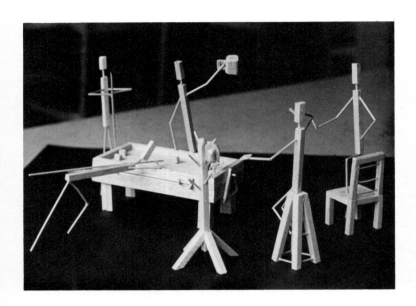

Stick figures are rarely believable, but these (by a junior high school student/artist) are, because of the fine gestures and details of action: a mug of beer raised, a player ready to shoot, a hat hanging on the rack.

A stuffed bear advertising furs is certainly a startling contrast to the ordinary. There is also contrast between the humor of a bear selling goods and the tragedy of a magnificent animal being humiliated, even after his death.

Comb, Vija Celmins. Enamel on wood, permission to photograph by Los Angeles County Museum of Art. An ordinary object like this comb, when seen as a giant work of art, sets up a contrast that is fascinating and difficult to ignore.

Contrast: Art Elements

LINE, FORM, COLOR, TEXTURE

Since so much contrast exists, perhaps it is more important to see ways that line, form, color and texture work to visually excite or please our eye.

Basic colors and triangular forms contrast in a harmony of strength and, at the same time, peacefulness. Photography by Walt Selleck.

Since contrasts through color are endless, let's limit ourselves on the color pages of this section to *yellow* and a few of the things it can do for a scene or work of art.

Here, yellow is seen simply as the color of a major company trademark. Below, yellow becomes a strong background, contrasting well with the blacks, reds and silver of the motorcycle. (Also see pages 38-39). Compare this color photo to the black and white version on page 27.

Rugged rocks contrast with rolling water, calm skies and boats in a highly textured scene.

Varied lines and their shadows are seen at a beach play area and in the construction of a new home.

Beyond Focus, oil on masonite, Josef Albers (1969). Collection, the Los Angeles County Museum of Art, promised gift of Mr. and Mrs. Taft Schreiber.

CONTRAST WITH YELLOW

Let's see how *yellow* works in a more complicated way in three famous paintings. Josef Albers' painting (opposite page) uses contrasts of yellow squares on top of each other to set up a variety of visual sensations—edges are hard and soft, the yellows push and pull and also intersect and blend—endless possibilities, through the relationship of color. Gaze at it for a few moments and see if these sensations exist for you.

Miro's painting contrasts flowing lines with bold forms of pure color. The interesting black, red, green and yellow forms stabilize the lively lines. For example, note how the strong yellow form at the bottom of the picture almost becomes a base for the other forms and lines to visually "rest on" or from which to "spring upward".

The yellow in Matisse's more naturalistic garden scene is used to help evoke the mood of a pleasant day. Interesting contrasts exist—the shoe of one lady dangles ordinarily while her face is distorted in a more "modern" way. Matisse also contrasted his use of paint and brush strokes—thick, thin, quick, stroked, blended, thereby capturing the textures and atmosphere.

Animated Forms, oil on canvas, Joan Miro (1935). Collection, the Los Angeles County Museum of Art, bequest of David E. Bright.

Tea, oil on canvas, Henri Matisse. Collection, the Los Angeles County Museum of Art, bequest of David L. Loew in memory of his father, Marcus Loew.

39

Contrast in Animals and Nature

Photograph courtesy of Los Angeles Zoo.

Contrasts can exist on animals for protection (spots), for function (sleek body for swimming) or simply because nature took its course. Many contrasts exist in nature—colors, lines, textures, shapes and forms. The contrasts may be dramatic, like the zebra's stripes, or subtle, like the varied blues of a calm body of water.

This large oil painting by a college student abstractly suggests clouds, water, land and leaves, as well as the motion of nature.

This photo, by a student, of a lone white horse contrasting with the scenery was shot with a "soft-focus" technique to give the photo a lyrical, romantic look. Photography by Debbie Selleck.

A soft, furry cat sniffs at a smooth, metal pitcher. Photography by Mary Selleck.

Masses of orange ladybugs contrast effectively against the greenery. Photography by Walt Selleck.

A simple garden of flowers can provide gorgeous colors and interesting and varied shapes.

All tree trunks are not alike—notice the variety of little
growths and colors on this one.

Untitled 1955, John D. McLaughlin. Oil on masonite, 32'' x 38''. Los Angeles County Museum of Art, Los Angeles County Funds.

44

Contrast Among Like Things

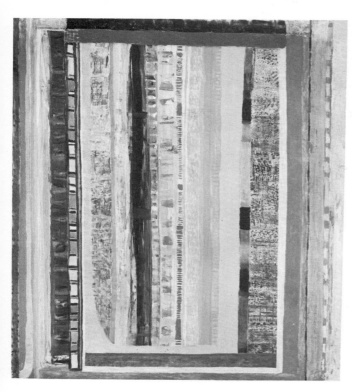

Untitled 1963, Robert Natkin. Oil on canvas, 50" x 60". Los Angeles County Museum of Art. Gift of Mrs. Vicci Sperry, through Contemporary Art Council.

Clean, minimal, precise rectangles. Dabbled, varied, textured rectangles. Rectangles reflecting rectangles. Different senses of space and mood.

A simple scene of grapefruit on a wall—contrasting in size, color and texture from "new green" to molding brown.

Artist Judith Lea Kunda does colorful wall or ceiling hangings. Controlled flat rectangles on one side contrast with the freer, spontaneous, multicolored rectangles on the other side. This is accomplished by allowing the colors to "bleed through" to the "looser side" until the fabric pores are filled with paint on the other side.

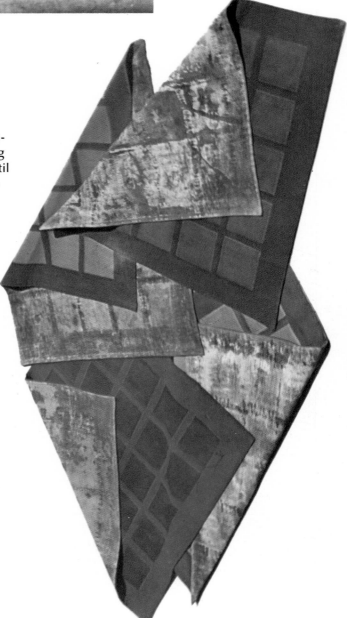

A collage face takes on a mysterious effect, partly because of the contrasting natural profile "face-within-a-face." Can you find the front view candelabra nose next to the profile view of lips? Junior high student work.

In some of the Chicano areas of East Los Angeles, artists of all ages have brightened the buildings and walls with murals, ranging from typical Mexican motifs to contemporary concepts.

The protective gate, when closed behind the window of this dress shop, accidentally becomes part of the triangular design of shapes and patterns of the clothing.

Something as simple as a trip to the market can become a visual adventure. Similar shaped items, when displayed with care, can present patterns of colorful and tactile pleasure.

Because the wallboard behind the wooden supports has loosened and warped, a strange contrast exists between the straight supports and their wavy shadows.

This rug is divided into varied shapes and is based on a design found in nature—the agate stone. By changing angles and directions, the repeated agate pattern remains visually exciting. Courtesy Edward Fields Inc. Photography by J. B. Esakoff

This museum, based on Roman architecture, contrasts three-dimensional columns with columns painted on the wall.

Reflections in the glass and water repeat but change shapes in this shopping plaza scene.

Contrasts in the City

Empty streets—a noise echoing. "Closed" signs in windows—"Go Away!" Busy streets—noises deafening. Signs flashing—"Come on in!" Billboards with ten foot cigarettes high above tiny people laughing, frowning, disappearing into shiny, new glass buildings. Old brick buildings caught between the present and the past. The City—*Contrasts*.

The contrast of many lines—thin wires, poles, railings, thick metal steps and their various angles—silhouetted against the sky.

The underground parking lot wall with an open design allows light to come through and brighten what would otherwise be a depressing darkness.

The clothes, clean and blowing in the wind, contrast with the time-worn, dark buildings.

Interesting contrasts exist in this photograph. The wall of the building is divided into four sections. The lettering in the upper left and the painting in the upper right suggest activity, but the lower left shows "Closed" and "For Rent" signs. The lower right is empty, providing a background for the woman walking by. A humorous contrast exists between the woman and the large, booted legs as they seem to have passed each other.

Many vertical and horizontal lines repeated in different shapes and patterns.

The lighted fountain and building contrast with the black sky.

City scene. A watercolor by a high school student. The brush is used in many contrasting ways to evoke the power and movement of a busy city.

It doesn't have to be "great art" or, for that matter, art at all in order to spark our imagination, give us ideas for our own work or just make us react—perhaps through a good laugh.

The "glob design" used on this car has little artistic value but will gain attention and promote business because of the shocking contrast to normal cars.

A huge nose is placed between two windows (eyes?) and the decoration over the door becomes the moustache as this little neighborhood playhouse is transformed into a large face.

The painted foreground figures seem to be discussing the "lady" statuettes. Many contrasts are seen: painted-unpainted, light-shadows, large figures-small figures.

Where there is activity, contrasts exist—people, clothing, signs, buildings and shapes of all kinds.

The artist or designer wants your attention! Often he uses contrast to get it. This clothing store uses a bold black and white letter contrast. The strong, black, angled area almost seems to say, "We're with it! Come on in!"

Sometimes people, objects or things get together and amuse or startle the viewer. The modern sculpture and the tractor make an incongruous pair, while the bird and man seem to have met before. Film-makers use this technique, sometimes in serious moments, often in comedies—"the cat who makes the burglar sneeze." An artist might do the same thing—surprise us with interesting combinations of shapes or unique color choices.

Contrast: Compositional Space and Balance

Some artists and photographers are interested in the sense of space that the canvas or nature offers. Locating objects or shapes in a painting or photograph can result in some dramatic spatial and balance concepts. Sam Francis' painting (opposite) is called *Towards Disappearance* and there *is* an effect of shapes floating, falling, moving away.

A lone tree contrasting against the canyon expanse emphasizes the great space.

60

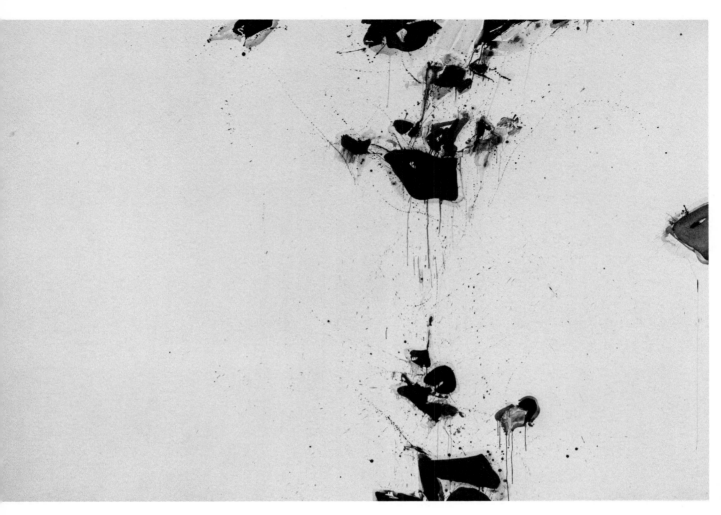

Towards Disappearance 1957, Sam Francis. Oil on canvas, 144″ x 108″. Los Angeles County Museum of Art, Gift of Contemporary Art Council.

Most of the objects in this college student's still life are placed in the left and left center of the canvas. However the knife, lemon and table leg in the lower right hold the picture in visual balance.

The rope lies against the sand—a thin line, moving to the sea. Birds and boats appear small in the distance. Light falls on the sand in certain areas. Many contrasts add to the sense of space.

This photo was "cropped" to dramatically contrast the figure in the lower right with the basket. The thin, vertical shape of the picture adds a visual tension as well as a sense of space.

The party's over! The photographer leaves a large area of lawn before the table in the background. Set back alone, with the table cloth blowing in the wind, it seems truly left and forgotten.

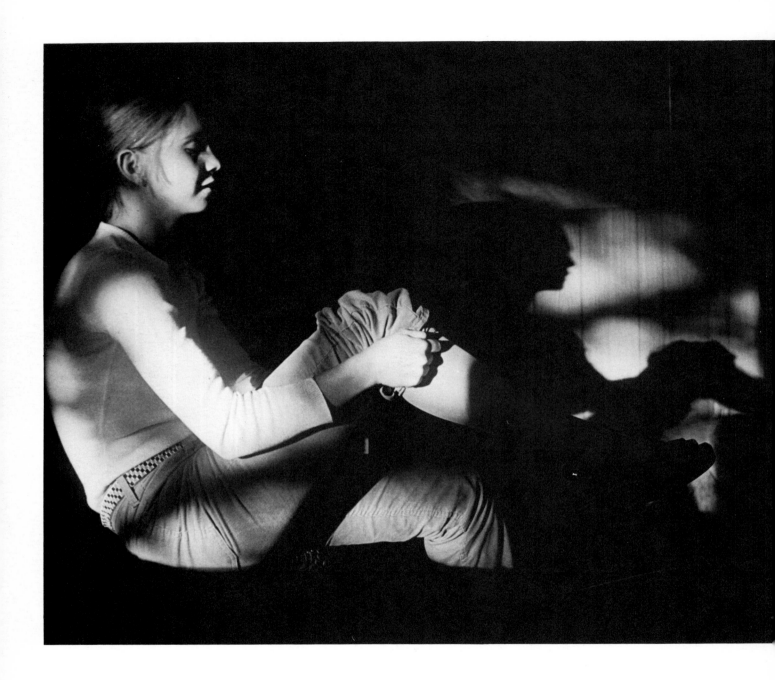

Contrast: Light and Dark

Exciting examples of light and shadow contrasts are all around us. As we get dressed with the early morning light spreading into our room, we glance out the window and see the beauty of light and shadow on the trees. As we ride in the car, we can see the variety and differences of the light and dark inside the car, contrasting with that outside.

A paint rag, dirty and stiff from dried paint, is transformed into a dramatic and beautiful form as sunlight plays on the surface of folds and wrinkles.

A piece of outdoor carpeting, tossed over a chair to dry, takes on the appearance of a ghostly, hooded figure, because of the strong contrasts of dark and light.

The various thicknesses and heights of these tree roots allow the sun and shadows to arrange a strong composition.

Portrait of a Man ca 1900, John Singer Sargent (Attrib.).
Los Angeles County Museum of Art, Mira T. Hershey
Memorial Collection.

For hundreds of years, artists, whether working
naturalistically or abstractly, have been interested in the
effects of dark and light and their dramatic possibilities.
Knowledge of dark and light and the skill to present it
are shown in this fine painting by Sargent.

Have you ever walked under a pier in the early morning
or late afternoon sun? Repeated shapes or objects,
when seen in strong dark and light, can present striking
patterns.

ARTIFICIAL LIGHT

Artificial light is used in many ways—to light a work of art, to guide us at night, as seen in the photograph of the exterior wall of a library, and even as a medium in creating a work of art.

Artists use artificial light in their work, from simple light bulbs to laser beams. Artist Dan Flavin combines fluorescent lights with daylight to create interesting visual sensations that incorporate the gallery space itself as part of the art work.

Untitled, Dan Flavin. Daylight, warm white fluorescent light. Wall #1: 12'' x 96''. Wall #2: 34'' x 96''. Photo courtesy Leo Castelli Gallery, N.Y. Photography by Eric Pollitzer.

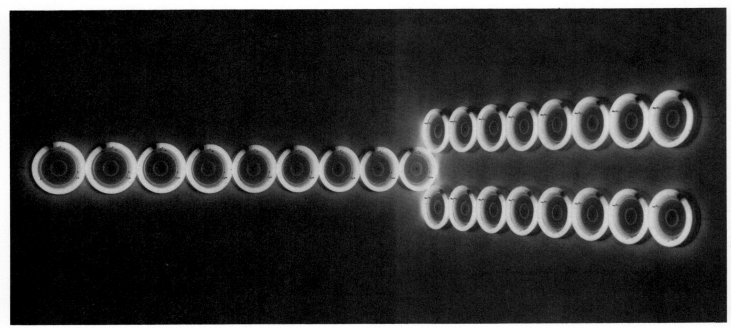

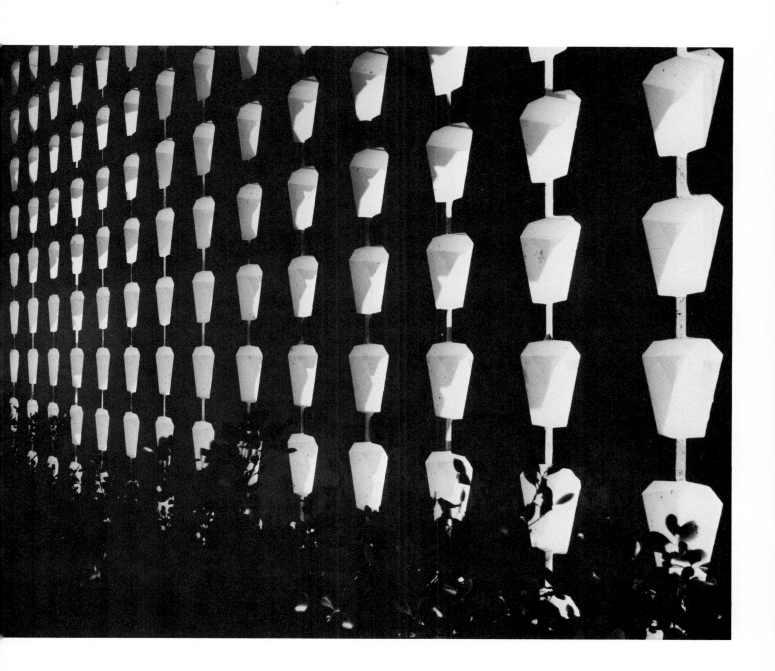

Contrast in Time and Motion

A work of art can actually move (for instance, a mobile or a motor driven sculpture) or it can appear to move through techniques used by the artist—angles, directions, color sensations. Sometimes, as the viewer moves, the artwork appears to move. Time can also be a factor in our viewing or doing. We remember . . . time changes things . . . and we can even see what might be as time passes. We can anticipate.

Models of prehistoric beasts momentarily send us back into time.

Years stand before our eyes in the form of a modern building contrasting with the form of an old church structure. Major differences in style, simplicity and details are obvious.

An often used project can still be an exciting way to experiment with contrast. The two pictures at right are of the same work of art. Developed around an "accordion effect," the picture changes visually as the viewer walks by. The same principle is used for some moving billboards.

A hillside of daisies. Some, just buds eager to open . . . others fully grown and stretching to the sun . . . while still others have already wilted. A composite of time.

Photographers can record for us the passing of our time. A perky, young girl, playing with her dog, becomes a young woman, less certain and somewhat shy. Then she becomes an attractive grandmother and watches her grandchildren playing with their dog and growing into young men and women.

Three photographs were superimposed and the lighting, angles and transition of flat planes penetrating each other add up to a sense of movement.

76

The field has been plowed, but the curving furrows remain as a reminder of the action that created them.

These two photographs are of the same moving sculpture by Jerome Kirk. It is called "Broken Circle." The arc form rising from the base contrasts with the "closed" circle but becomes more like parts of the "broken" circle. Many other contrasts exist as this sculpture moves and changes.

Index

A junior high school student's block print landscape has a wonderful rhythm of movement because of the varied lines that follow the objects and areas they describe. Lines run up the trees and over the hills and into the clouds. The black and white contrast strengthens this visual sensation.

Acknowledgments

I want to thank the many people who helped me during the progress of this book. Philippa Calnan and Nancy Reid of the Los Angeles County Museum of Art gave generously of their time in order to provide photographs for my use.

Editor Jerry Brommer was, as usual, most knowledgeable and eager to be of assistance.

The professional and student artists and photographers represented, and the galleries and business firms that contributed their encouragement, as well as photographic material, are greatly appreciated.

It is quite possible that without the many hours of work put forth by my brother Walt, who developed the negatives and prints, the book might not have been completed — certainly not on time.

I am grateful to Craig Singerman, a student at Emerson Junior High School, for typing the manuscript, and to Sue Quinn for proofreading.

Thanks again to my wife and daughter, not only for their encouragement, but also for enduring a year of LINE and a year of CONTRAST.

All photographs were taken by the author unless otherwise acknowledged.